How Well Do You Know Me

1000 Questions for Couple

Copyright © 2021

All rights reserved.

DEDICATION

The author and publisher have provided this e-book to you for your personal use only. You may not make this e-book publicly available in any way. Copyright infringement is against the law. If you believe the copy of this e-book you are reading infringes on the author's copyright, please notify the publisher at: https://us.macmillan.com/piracy

How Well Do You Know Me

Contents

Introduction 1

Personality, Feelings & Emotions 3

Favorites 14

Pets 16

Attractions 18

Health, Food & Well Being 22

Vacations 28

Morals, Convictions and Beliefs 32

Religion & Spiritual Matters 36

Car & Driver 42

Past & Future 44

Love, Romance & Date Nights 46

Friends & Family 48

Conclusion 53

Introduction

Even if it seems like common sense to set clear expectations with your fiancé before getting married and starting a life together, it's surprising how many engaged couples think that being in love equals having the same set of values.

Very few couples know the right questions to ask before marriage. They falsely believe they are going to go through marriage together as husband and wife, just as harmoniously as they navigated their relationship in the beginning.

But marriage brings new obstacles and hurdles to relationships that can pop up after a happy engagement.

So, before you tie the knot and get married, it's important to sit down with your fiancé and ask each other deep questions about your past, present and future as a couple. You'll be glad you did.

How should you go about asking your future spouse these questions, and how should you respond to their questions for you?

Find a time when the two of you can sit together alone relaxed and without distractions or pressing concerns. You can make a fun evening of it and go through the entire list of questions below all at once, or take your time visiting the questions section by section over the course of a few days or weeks.

The purpose of these tough questions is to make sure you and your

How Well Do You Know Me

partner are on the same page, so the most important thing is to keep an open mind and approach both your own answers and those your partner gives from a place of authentic curiosity, honesty and trust.

Whether you've been together for years or perhaps not as long, you've probably never thought about discussing at least some of these topics together. These questions are meant to help you go deeper in your relationship, discover what you have in common (or don't), and if you really are a good fit for one another.

If you're already engaged, now is a great time to ask each other these questions, but it's even better if you and your partner have a serious relationship, want to have the talk about marriage, and are considering taking the next step.

Be sure to keep an open mind, an open heart, and be willing to get to know your partner on another level.

Here are 1000 questions to ask before marriage that will affect your future together as husband and wife.

Personality, Feelings & Emotions

This is by far the largest collection of questions and rightly so. Your personality is the heart and core of who you are. You might be able to change your viewpoints on religion, sex and politics but how you react to tragedies and triumphs will rarely be different from year to year. Answers to these questions will give you insight into your partner and will fill you with a deeper understanding of who they are.

What things about me remind you of anyone from your past, either past sweethearts or good friends?

What do you think are my talents? Do you think you have any of the same talents?

How many physical fights have you been in? Do you usually start them? Why do you fight?

Has anyone very dear to you died? How did you handle it?

What are you most fearful of? How does that fear keep you from doing things you would like to do?

Are you chirpy in the morning or are you a grouch?

Do you ever pick up hitchhikers? Which type of people would you pick up?

How often do you think your gut feeling is correct? When can you remember that it was incorrect?

How Well Do You Know Me

What one skill do you wish you had learned but haven't yet (Play the piano? Learn a foreign language? Fly a plane? Etc.)?

Does public speaking frighten you? Have you had much experience with it?

What sort of reaction do you have when you get very upset?

Is it ever appropriate for someone to express anger in a physical way? If so, when and how?

How do typically handle the trauma from a big loss whether it is from the death of a loved one, getting fired or some other big disappointment?

What is your typical reaction when someone criticizes you?

About what things are you most selfish?

Do you think that you are able to calmly and wisely react in emergencies? What are some examples of emergencies you have had?

How did you feel when a beloved pet of yours died?

Do you have a dream that repeats again and again? What is it?

What feeling do you have the most difficulty controlling?

What feeling do you have the most difficulty expressing?

How do you think I handle myself when I'm in a crisis situation?

If you could choose to know everything about one topic, what area

How Well Do You Know Me

would you choose to be an expert?

How would someone be able to tell if you're happy? If you're sad?

Are you an organized person?

If a fire destroyed your home and all of your belongings, what would you do? If you could take out three things before the blaze, what would they be? (Assuming there is no one in the house at the time of the fire.)

If you were a very talented writer and were guaranteed to sell 100,000 copies of whatever book you wrote, what would it be about?

Does any particular season make you happier than others? If so, do you know why?

Do you like your first name? Have you ever wished you had a different name? What name would it be?

When you are sick and feeling poorly, do you like to be alone or do you like to be pampered and have someone close to your side most of the time?

What is the most thoughtful, caring thing you have ever done?

Do you ever think that your partner gives more time, love and affection to a child or pet and it makes you jealous?

Do you like to exaggerate things for effect?

If you had to be a different nationality, what country would you like to have been born in? Why?

How Well Do You Know Me

If you were given $50,000 to throw a party for all of your friends, what sort of party would you put together?

Are you a morning, a night person or somewhere in the middle?

Do you think you would prefer a calm, loving, consistent marriage or one that was full of excitement, wild times and rocky patches?

Do you think you are a fairly typical man/woman in the way you think, act and believe?

Are you one who adapts to change easily? Can you cite some examples?

Do you have a child's heart sometimes? What sort of "childish" things do you think about doing?

Are you generally an optimist, pessimist or a realist?

How often do you cry? What situations often bring you to tears? What makes you feel secure and safe?

Do you tend to analyze your decisions before you talk about them or do ideas and thoughts blurt out without much forethought?

Would you describe yourself as a peace-keeper or a trouble-maker?

What type of social gatherings do you prefer - small groups or large parties?

Do you like to be the life of the party or do you prefer intimate, one on one conversation?

How Well Do You Know Me

Are you more of an introvert or an extrovert? Does it change depending on the crowd?

Do you experience PMS? Is it mild or severe? How does your mood change and for how many days? How do you want to be treated during your period?

What do you tend to be humble about? When do you catch yourself being arrogant?

Do you tend to keep a lot of thoughts and feelings to yourself or do you share them pretty openly?

Do you ever lose your temper? How does it manifest itself?

Do you give money to homeless people/beggars? Why or why not?

What experiences usually make you filled with joy?

Do you currently believe that you are mature and experienced enough to be able to build and maintain a very successful marriage? When did you feel you were ready or when do you think you will be there?

Which do you think should have the final say in decisions - logic or emotions? Why?

In what circumstances do you feel most at peace?

Men, what do you think is the best thing about being a guy? Women, what do you think is the best thing about being a female?

Do you think of yourself as mechanically inclined?

How Well Do You Know Me

If you were given the opportunity to successfully run for president, would you do so? When you won, what three things would you most like to improve in your country?

If someone gave you one million dollars that you were required to give to some person or organization, who would you give it to?

Do you enjoy hugging people? Do you like receiving hugs?

What five things have you done in your life that you are most proud of?

Tell me about the most emotional cry that you can recall.

Has there ever been a time when you felt like you were going to "lose it"?

If your partner had an affair, how would you react? Could you forgive him or her?

If your partner had a one-night fling after drinking too much, how would you react? Could you forgive him or her?

Are you able to keep secrets? Is it hard for you?

Have you ever given a speech? What was the last one about?

Does anyone give you an inferiority complex?

Do you think that luck has much to play in your life?

Do you find it difficult to compromise on things?

How Well Do You Know Me

Do you have a fear of being alone? Rejected? Unloved?

Is there anything that makes you feel homesick, nostalgic or sentimental?

Do you have an idol? Do you try to model yourself after him or her in some way?

Do you think of yourself more as a leader or a follower?

Over the last five years how do you think you have changed for the worse? Better?

Did you have a point in your life where you turned your life around?

What one thing could you change in your behavior that would make your relationship closer? What is keeping you from making that change?

Is there anything that you constantly worry about?

If someone tells you a juicy tidbit about a friend or coworker, do you have difficulty keeping it to yourself? Do you ever tell people they shouldn't gossip?

If you were paid a salary to work for any one charity for an entire year, which charity would you choose?

Would you rather be mute, blind or deaf? Which of the three would be the worst?

Is there anything that you have practically no self-control over (ice

How Well Do You Know Me

cream, offers for a roll in the hay, a bargain shoe sale, a beanie baby for your collection, etc.)?

Do you think you are interesting or a bore?

Are you more sensitive than most people of your gender?

Do you usually ask for help or support or do you prefer to fail all on your own?

If you had huge financial losses and had to liquidate all of your possessions including your car and home, what would that do to your self-esteem?

What makes you feel important?

How would you rate your maturity among your peers?

What is your number one flaw? What steps are you taking to overcome it?

Do you see yourself as worthy of love? Why or why not?

What is your greatest disappointment?

Have you ever worked really hard at something but it didn't pay off in the end?

Do you have a "special place"? Why is it so meaningful to you?

Why do you feel that you are trustworthy?

Do you think you are competitive? In what areas?

How Well Do You Know Me

Am I a nagger? How so? Does it irritate you?

Are there any rituals you do every day?

How do you feel when someone close to you disagrees with you?

In which areas of your life do you feel like you are an independent?

In which areas are you dependent on others?

Do you enjoy debating others?

In what ways do you feel really blessed?

What things tend to make you angry? How do you usually react when you are angry?

On which topics do you feel qualified at giving advice?

Would you make a serious attempt to lose weight if your partner asked you to?

How do you think I could enjoy life more?

What is a talent that you wish you possessed?

Do you write important dates such as birthdays and anniversaries in your calendar? Do you use a calendar? Do you usually remember those dates?

Have you ever played any musical instruments? Which ones and do you still play them?

If you had to be famous, what would you want to be famous for? Do

How Well Do You Know Me

you think fame would be a good thing or a bad thing for your relationship?

If you knew you would die in two days, how would you spend the time until then?

How many hours does it take until you can't stand being alone anymore?

What makes life worth living?

Do you think I am a lot like the other members of my family? How am I like them?

What are your thoughts on crying?

Can you think of any trait of mine that reminds you of your father or mother?

Are you a balanced person? If so, how did you get to be balanced? If not, what steps do you need to take to be more balanced?

If you could make any three changes to our school systems, what would they be?

If you could live one year of your life all over again without changing a thing, what year would you choose? Why?

Do you prefer receiving expensive gifts or ones that come from the heart?

How Well Do You Know Me

Do you know most of your neighbors? Do you ever socialize with any of them?

Have you ever lived alone? Do you or did you enjoy it?

Someone once said "A women who does not feel loved needs jewelry, gold and dazzling gifts to be happy. A woman who truly feels loved finds those gifts to be superfluous (nice, but not necessary)".

Do you agree?

Prior to this year, what is the best gift you've ever received? Why was it so special?

How do feel about your mate reading your private email?

Are you camera shy? Why?

Do you feel that you need to be occasionally held or emotionally supported by someone who is strong? Why or why not?

Do you generally make to do lists? Would you like it or be offended if your mate helped you make a to do list?

Do you feel like you waste a lot of time? Do you wish you didn't? Do you feel that your partner wastes a lot of time? Does that bother you?

Do you tend to be punctual or are you usually late?

What are some things that you consider a waste of time?

What do you like most about my personality?

Favorites

You will find this section to be invaluable when it comes time to celebrate a special occasion or to just let someone know they are special. Put your sweetheart's answers on file somewhere and refer back to it often.

Do you have a favorite type (or a couple) of music? A favorite singer? Or musical group?

What is your favorite fast food restaurant? How often do you eat there?

What's your favorite restaurant for casual dining? Favorite special occasion restaurant?

Do you remember what your favorite childhood books were?

Do you have a favorite movie? Actor? Actress? Comedy? Drama?

What's your favorite alcoholic beverage?

What meal would you eat most often if you could?

Do you have a favorite "fancy" meal?

What is your favorite snack food? Dessert?

What's your favorite ice cream flavor?

Do you have a favorite and least favorite day of the week? Why do you feel that way?

How Well Do You Know Me

What is your favorite time of day?

What's your favorite candy bar?

What is your favorite ethnic cuisine?

Pets

Too many people put too little thought into pet ownership. It's not quite as serious as having children, but it is not that far off. Having certain pets will affect many areas of your relationship: money, vacations, careers and even holiday celebrations. Pets can be expensive and make it difficult to go away for vacations (or even out to dinner right after work). But for some, they are well worth the sacrifices.

If you could have any pets you wanted and had the space and money to properly care for them, what pets would you want to have?

Are you allergic to animals? If your fiancé was allergic to your pets, would you be willing to give them away to a good home?

Are there any types of pets that you refuse to live with (snakes, rats, stray dogs, etc.)?

Do you allow your pets to be on the furniture?

Do you get your pets "fixed" or do you allow them to keep producing litters? What do you do with the babies?

Are there any circumstances where you think it is a good idea to put animals "to sleep"?

Do you think that it is cruel to keep a dog in a cage or tied up most of the time?

How do you feel about dogs that are bred to attack and have been

How Well Do You Know Me

known to kill children (Pit Bulls, Rotweillers)?

Do you feed your pets food off of your plate? How do you feel about that practice?

Do you take your pets with you on short trips? Long vacations? Do you put them in a kennel or have a friend watch them?

Do you have a preference for cats or dogs? Indoor pets vs. outdoor pets?

If you get a pet for your children and they don't take care of it, who will be responsible for cleaning up after it, feeding it and walking it?

How do you feel about getting dogs professionally groomed?

If you and your mate purchased a pet and later split up, how do you think you would decide who got the pet?

How do you feel about pets being in the bedroom or sleeping on your bed?

Attractions

They say beauty is only skin deep, but that skin certainly has a way of making men and women swoon and fawn. Red hair, great smiles, kind eyes, full figures and a whole myriad of features are responsible for causing men and women to come a little bit closer. Others find the way you talk, walk, or dress to be magnetic. Some people fall in love with the way someone looks, others fall in love with what is beneath the skin.

If you didn't like your mate's clothing or hairstyle, would you tell him or her? Would you want your partner to tell you?

What first attracted you to me? How has that one attraction changed since then?

If you went bald, would you consider wearing a toupee or getting hair plugs?

Would you want your spouse to talk with you first before they dramatically changed their hairstyle or facial hair?

If your partner asked you to shave or not to shave (face, underarms, legs, pubic area) would you do it? What is your preference for shaving those areas?

If you had problems with my personal hygiene, would you be able to tell me?

How Well Do You Know Me

What physical or personality trait do you think makes people first attracted to you?

Do stylish clothes, nice hair, expensive jewelry or "things" make you feel better about yourself?

Do you think you tend to attract a certain type of person? Do you feel like you need to dress sexy? Why or why not?

Do you feel that people who dress sexy are sending the message that they are interested in sex?

How do you feel about permanent tattoos? Why do you think most people get them?

If you suddenly became blind, how would your idea of the perfect mate change?

Do you believe in love at first sight? If so, what about the millions of cases when love at first site ended in disaster?

Do you really like the way I dress? What changes could I make that would please you?

Which do you think you would rather have: a gorgeous mate who wasn't very interested in sex or very good in bed or a very ordinary looking spouse that was awesome in the sack?

If you could be any height and build you desire, what would it be?

Should your sweetheart love you just the way you are, or would you be willing to make some changes (the way you dress, shaving, new hairstyle, etc) to become more attractive to him or her?

In what ways are you smart?

How would you feel if your mate wanted to wear matching outfits or dress like you?

What do you find attractive about my physical features? Is there a favorite?

If you were single and wanted to write a personal ad describing your qualities, how would it read?

Do you fear looking older?

How do you feel about women wearing makeup? What do you think is ideal?

What is your opinion on women spending money to get their nails done? Do you have a preference on how you like women's nails?

What do you perceive to be your physical flaws?

Are you currently comfortable with your body? If not, what would you change to make you comfortable?

How would you feel if I had breast implants?

If you could change one thing about your body, what would it be?

What outfit of mine is your favorite? Why is it?

Do you think that dressing is something you do out of necessity or do

How Well Do You Know Me

you enjoy putting outfits together?

If your aunt left you a large sum of money in her will for you to have any sort of plastic surgery you desired would you have anything done?

Name one or two minor changes I could make to my appearance that would make me more attractive?

Health, Food & Well Being

Some people want to eat, drink, smoke and be merry while others want to eat lean, drink moderately, exercise and be healthy. For many people, how they take care (or don't take care) of themselves is part of their "lifestyle." It dictates how early they wake up, what friends they hang out with, what they do for entertainment and even how they vacation. Poor mental and/or physical health can put limitations on what the two of you will be able to do as a couple, especially as you get older. It is no small thing to consider.

Do you have any phobias, fears or concerns about going to the doctor?

Do you have any concerns over vaccinations or flu shots for you or your children?

What are your feelings about recreational drugs? Have you ever taken any and if so, how long did you use drugs? Do you still use them?

Do you have any concerns about my health or unhealthy habits?

Second hand smoke is one of the leading causes of cancer and breathing related illnesses. Will you allow anyone to smoke around your children? If you smoke now would you make a serious attempt to quit before having children?

Have you ever suffered from depression (not just feeling blue, but a feeling of extreme sadness that leaves you nearly paralyzed)? If so, what brought these feelings on, how long did the depression last and what therapies worked for you?

Have you ever had serious thoughts about committing suicide? What are your thoughts about those who kill themselves?

Do you think tobacco should be banned since it is an addictive drug? If that happened what affect would it have on people's lives 20 years from now? Should marijuana be made legal? How would that change affect society 20 years from now?

When, if ever, was the first time you smoked a cigarette? Why did you try it? How long did you smoke? If you still smoke, have you ever seriously tried to quit?

Do you smoke (or chew tobacco)? How often? How long have you been doing so and have you ever tried to stop? What methods?

Which meals would you like to be able to eat together? Do you think we will be able to consistently do so?

Do you get irritated when you have to wait in long lines? Will you wait 45 minutes to be seated in a restaurant?

Do you have any special dietary needs? How do you need me to support you with this need?

Do you consider yourself in shape?

Do you live to eat or eat to live?

How Well Do You Know Me

What do you think are your optimum hours of sleep to be fully energized?

Do you ever diet? What sort of diets do you usually go on?

How often do you get sick? Is it a cold, flu or usually something else?

Are you a coupon collector? Do you sometimes get fanatical about saving money on groceries?

How many drinks does it take until you are definitely "feeling it." Do you cut yourself off after a certain number of drinks? Or when do you know you have had enough?

Have you ever had an emotional breakdown or been diagnosed with a mental illness? How long did the recovery take?

What do you think about eating meals (with your family) in front of the television?

Do you think family time and discussions around the dinner table are important?

Do you have any rooms that are off limits for bringing in food?

Do you find that you eat when you are bored, stressed, or worried? Are there emotional times that make you want to eat?

Have you ever deliberately thrown up food or ate tiny amounts of food to lose weight?

How much time per day/week do you currently exercise? How much time do you think you should spend? How do you think we could help each other with our exercise regimens?

Do you have any particular health concerns (e.g. heart problems, high blood pressure, diabetes, asthma, etc.)?

Do you get a regular medical checkup? When was your last one?

Are you more likely to take over the counter medicines, prescription medicines, homeopathic medicines, natural remedies or nothing at all when you are sick?

Do you cook or do you only eat prepackaged food? How often do you go out to eat?

Will you eat everything on your plate no matter how much is there (assuming you like the food)? Or will you quit when you feel full enough? Do you need to feel "stuffed" to be satisfied?

What form of exercise do you prefer?

Do you currently suffer from a sleeping disorder? Have you ever?

Do you enjoy eating leftovers? Do you refuse to eat leftovers?

Do you always like to sample your partner's food in restaurants? Does it bother you if someone always wants to taste your food/drink?

Have you ever done any stupid or dangerous things when you were drunk? Like what?

Do you regularly take vitamins? Do you think the foods you eat have enough naturally occurring vitamins in them?

Could you ever be married to someone whose breath and clothes always reeked of tobacco?

Do you try to eat healthy meals? Organic?

Are you currently on any medication? What for?

On average, how many alcoholic beverages do you have in a week? Is that all at once, on the weekend or spread about through the week? 25

Do you like to plan your week's menu in advance or cook whatever you are in the mood for (or have ingredients for)?

Do you enjoy cooking for company or do you feel inadequate?

Do you usually just buy what you need at the store, whatever is on sale, or whatever looks good?

Are you highly critical of the food and service when you dine out? Can you go out and enjoy a meal or do you always have to "rate" it?

Are you fearful of germs or food poisoning and tend to toss everything out of the refrigerator that is more than a week old?

Were you taught proper table manners growing up? Do you feel that your table manners need improving? Would you like for your mate to point out where you could improve? Do your partner's table manners embarrass you when you eat in public?

Do drink coffee? If so, how many times a week and how many cups each day? Do you feel that you need a caffeine "fix" to get going for the day?

Do you ever drink and drive? Would you agree not to if your partner had a big problem with you doing so? Do you have any allergies?

Have you been abused in any way - sexually, emotionally, or physically? Do you still have emotional scars from it? Have you ever counseled about it?

Are you a gourmet - enjoying trying all sorts of international cuisine or do you prefer to eat the same basic food all the time?

Do you remember your first alcoholic drink? What were the circumstances?

Who do you think should be responsible for grocery shopping and cooking in a marriage? When you are married how many times a week do you think you would eat out?

What foods do you really dislike? Are there any foods you don't eat for health or other reasons?

Have you ever been hospitalized? What for? What was the experience like?

Vacations

There are so many questions in this category probably because travel is a particular passion of my wife's and mine. It is such a delight to be able to spend weeks relaxing, exploring and soaking up the world's culture with someone who loves to travel in the same fashion as I do. I view all of our vacations as marriage retreats, a time and experience that draw us closer together.

Do you enjoy experiencing different ways of life or do you usually find it frustrating that they don't do things as efficiently or like the way things are done back home?

Have you ever traveled out of the country? Do you have a passport? When does it expire?

Do you usually do some business while you are on vacation (answering email, checking voicemail, returning phone calls, etc.)? How much time each day? Is that pretty much necessary?

Would you rather take a one-week $5000 vacation or would you rather go on three different one-week vacations that cost $1700 each?

What is the maximum length vacation you think you could take away from work without causing a problem? If you were retired or between jobs how long could you be away?

If you could plan any vacation for us, where would it be?

How Well Do You Know Me

When you travel, what is your usual goal (relax, sight see, see friends/family, do culture things, eat at new restaurants, etc.)?

Do you go back to the same places again and again or do you desire to go to new places most of the time when you travel?

Do you like to travel on the spur of the moment (hey, let's drive to the mountains next weekend)?

How many times during the year do you travel? How many times for business and how many pleasure vacations?

How much does your typical one week vacation cost (not including air fare)? Do you think you take budget vacations, moderate or expensive trips?

Do you fly as cheaply as possible or do you splurge for business or first class when going on vacation?

Do you tend to get sea sick or motion sick? What cures have you tried?

What was the best vacation you've ever taken?

Have you ever been on a group tour? What do you think about them?

Do you like to take vacations that are activity oriented (cycling trips, skiing trips, scuba trips, etc.)?

Do you enjoy camping? What eating/sleeping arrangements are tolerable?

Who looks after your home when you are away on vacation?

How Well Do You Know Me

How do you handle the language barrier when you travel to foreign countries? Are you willing to visit places where your language might not be spoken?

Do you think you would enjoy going on a vacation with your sweetheart's family? Would you detest it or do you not know them well enough to decide?

What are your thoughts on separate vacations? If we had limited income and different travel priorities, do you think we should take vacations without each other every once in a while?

When you go on a vacation with someone, do you like doing everything together, most things together or most things on your own and then getting back together for meals?

If you and your mate each have an income and maintain separate accounts, how do you split the costs of a vacation?

What sort of research, if any, do you do before you travel somewhere?

How do you feel about going on weekend getaways?

If you enjoy traveling, what places do you like to go to most often? Are there any places you have no desire to go to?

Do you arrive at the airport ahead of time in case problems arise or do you try to get there at the last possible minute so you don't have to wait?

How Well Do You Know Me

Do you save up for a vacation or do you put it all on credit and pay it off as you can?

How many weeks each year can you take off from work?

Morals, Convictions and Beliefs

Everyone has morals, convictions and beliefs. We just get them from different sources. Some follow a religious code to try to live a good life. Others are taught right and wrong from parents. Experiences, both good and bad, often help us to fashion our belief system. Some opposing viewpoints can dwell harmoniously under the same roof. Others will cause a lifetime of pain and friction.

If we ended up having opposite political views, how would that affect our relationship? Any particular issue you would find difficult to tolerate the opposite viewpoint?

Have you ever committed a felony? Have you ever been arrested?

Are you listed as an organ donor on your driver's license for when you die? Would you like for your organs to be donated?

Do you have a position on the government killing men and women who have knowingly committed murder?

What do you think about pornography? Do you think it is ever helpful?

How do you feel about men and women killing people from other countries? Have you already been in a war? How did it affect you to have to kill (or support those who killed) others?

Are you an activist for any causes?

Do you think you could kill a person if they were threatening the life

How Well Do You Know Me

of your loved ones?

Would you be able to marry someone who formerly was in a gay relationship or had a few homosexual experiences prior to dating you?

Is there anyone you would be willing to die for? Do you vote regularly?

Do you vote straight Republican, Democrat or other party? Or do you analyze each candidate and vote for who you think is most qualified regardless of party affiliation?

Are you currently involved in any criminal activities right now?

Would you steal a car for $200,000 if you would be certain that you would not be caught? What about for $1,000,000?

How would you feel if one of your friends said he or she was gay? Would you still want to socialize with him or her?

Are you often embarrassed about how most of your race behaves? Do you think your race is superior to all others/most?

How do you feel about gambling? If your company sent you on a business trip to Las Vegas, what limit would you place on yourself for gambling each day?

To what extent are you involved in politics? How do you feel about having guns in your home?

Do you have guidelines regarding movies you will not see?

Do you use foul language? Why do you do it? Does it bother you when

How Well Do You Know Me

you hear others cuss?

Is there anything you would physically fight for?

If you found a wallet with $300 cash in it, would you return it to its owner? Would you turn it into the police if there was no identification in it?

Do you feel strongly against people wearing fur coats?

Are you liberal, conservative or somewhere in the middle?

Do you think your parents are/were racist? How did that affect the way you think about people of other races?

From your past relationships, do you think that most people learn from their mistakes or do they simply keep repeating them?

Do you believe that most people are trustworthy and honest?

Tell me about the biggest lie you've ever told? Why did you tell it and how did you feel afterwards?

What do you do to protect the environment? Do you think you should do more?

Do you think you could go skinny dipping with your mate in private? How about with a group of people you knew?

Have you ever been to or would you ever go to a nude beach? What is your opinion on nudism (people who enjoy being nude around others - not in a sexual way)?

How Well Do You Know Me

Besides traffic violations, have you ever knowingly broken a law? What did you do?

Do you believe that there are some laws that aren't necessary to be kept?

Do you support (with money and/or time) any charities or causes?

If your dear friends wanted you to donate sperm or eggs because they were infertile, would you do so? How would you feel about your mate doing so? What about donating them for a couple that would remain anonymous?

Do you believe there is one right person for you out there in the world or that there can be many different potential mates that you could live blissfully with?

What sort of emotions (rage, anger, sorrow, etc.) do you think are inappropriate for people to express publicly?

What are your thoughts on handguns that serve no other real purpose than shooting people?

Have you ever stolen anything? Why? Were you caught?

Religion & Spiritual Matters

Religion and politics are the two things, it is said, which should not be brought up at dinner because they can be so divisive. People have given their lives for both. Since many people feel so strongly about religion (after all, to some people their eternal life depends upon it), it is definitely worth discussing at length with the person you might spend the rest of your entire life with. Since the vast majority of those who will buy this book are of the Christian faith, several questions are addressed to them.

Do you think astrological birth signs represents ones character? Why?

Do you believe in God? What were you raised to believe about religion?

If you are a Christian, what does the word "submission" in Ephesians 5:21,22 mean?

How do you feel that a husband can "submit" in marriage?

Do you believe all religions are worshipping God the way He wants us to?

What has been your most negative experience with your religion or other religions? What has been your most positive experience with your religion or other religions?

If you are turned off on religion is it because of bad experiences you

How Well Do You Know Me

have had with humans or is it because you are unhappy with God?

Do you have any customs or rituals regarding celebrating births and remembering deaths in your family?

About how many times a month/year do you attend church services?

How important is religion when deciding to seriously date someone? What religious differences would cause you serious doubts about a long-term relationship?

Do you believe that if you give money to churches or charity that you will be financially rewarded? Rewarded in other ways?

Do you believe in ghosts, angels or extraterrestrial beings? Why?

If you have religious convictions regarding sex before marriage, what boundaries should you set up so you live up to those convictions?

If you say you are a religious person, do you really practice it? Have you studied your religion's doctrines? In which ways are you not actively following your faith?

Have you seriously studied other faiths besides your own? If you are a Christian do you know what other denominations believe and teach?

What doctrines are essential for a church to teach in order for you to be able to become a member?

Do you attend the church you were brought up in? Would you consider attending a different church/denomination if your spouse desired?

How Well Do You Know Me

Is it more important that you attend a church where you are comfortable or is it more important that you worship with your husband/children? What do you think of couples who each attend their own Christian church?

Could you marry someone who does not share your fundamental religious beliefs?

When we die, what do you think happens to us? What do you base your opinion on?

What do you think it means to receive Christ as your Savior and Lord or "have you been saved"?

Have you ever personally received Christ as your Savior and Lord? Yes/No/Unsure If yes, Where? When?

What would you like to happen to your body (buried, cremated, donated to science, etc.) when you die? Do you have this stipulation in writing anywhere?

What are your father's and mother's religious backgrounds?

If we practice different religions, what problems might that cause with our wedding, the way we celebrate holidays, and how we will raise our children?

Do you believe that mankind is created with free-will (the ability to make right or wrong decisions) or that everything in life is predestined (planned out for you)?

How Well Do You Know Me

Is there any way we could use religion to help fill our marriage with love and peace?

Do you want a church wedding. If so, why?

Do you believe that the Bible is the inspired Word of God? Why?

Do you have any religious, ethical or cultural reasons why you think people of different races should not marry?

How often do you pray? Why do you pray?

Do you have any superstitions? What are they?

The Bible emphatically states that eternal life only comes through belief in Jesus Christ and his sacrifice. If you are a Christian, how do you feel about living with someone who does not have the same hope of eternal life? What if they worshipped some other god than Jesus Christ?

If you and your mate had significantly different religious beliefs, what would you teach your children about God? Would you want your mate to teach your children things that contradict your beliefs?

Do you believe most people who convert to their mate's religion do so out of keeping peace in the family or because they sincerely understand and believe the tenets of their mate's faith? Does it matter?

Would you be willing to go through a workshop or class that discussed the basic beliefs and doctrines of your partner's church?

How does your faith help you cope with problems and trials?

How Well Do You Know Me

Are there evil spirits in the world? Do you fear them?

What place do you believe religion will have in our lives?

Is religion important in your daily life? Why or why not?

How to do feel about those who are in different religions? Do you believe that God has a plan to save the whole world from eternal death (those who want to be saved) or only those who hear and believe the "truth" in this lifetime?

Were you afraid of God as a child?

To what extend do you think God expects us to follow and obey religious leaders?

Does your religion have a policy on contraception? What is it?

If you don't go to church at all or very often, do you think that might change when you have children? Why wait until then?

Can you think of anything that might make you want to stop attending church?

Do you think God created rules and instructions (a religion) to help men keep close to him? Or do you think man just made up those rules?

Do you have spiritual yearnings? What questions to life are you trying to figure out?

How many hours a week do you typically devote to your religious practices (e.g. going to church, prayer meetings, bible study, etc.)?

How Well Do You Know Me

Do you believe in reincarnation?

Do you believe that the Satan of the Bible actually exists? If so, what is he doing? Why is he evil?

Which religions do you think are the most harmful and destructive?

Some people say they are "spiritual" but not "religious". What does that mean to you?

If you pray, what do you give thanks for and what do you ask for? Do you fear God? Why or why not?

Do you believe that God does anything that does not make sense? Can you always apply human logic to analyze religion?

If we currently attend the same church but years from now I lost interest and stopped attending, how do you think that might affect our marriage?

Why do you think the Bible states that Christians should meet regularly with other believers and worship Him?

Does your partner have any religious beliefs that you feel are plain wrong (not going to doctors, no birth control, animal sacrifices, not wearing make-up, etc.) and you will not go along with?

Car & Driver

This might seem like a silly category but considering that you are literally putting your life in someone else's hands each time you sit in the passenger seat, it is really very important. To many, vehicles are more than just a mode of transportation; they are like pets or children and are even given names.

Do you prefer to be the passenger or the driver? Are you a back seat driver?

What is your primary mode of transportation? Do you wish you had a different option?

Do you ride motorcycles? Do you wear a helmet when bicycling or motorcycling? Is it the law where you live?

Do you wear your seat belt when you are in a vehicle? If not, would you wear one if your mate asked you to because they love you?

Have you ever received a D.W.I./D.U.I.? How many and how long ago?

Do you currently hitchhike from time to time? Have you ever?

Do you let your friends drive your vehicle if they need one to run an errand? Would you let you mate drive it on a regular basis?

What do you feel is important in a vehicle for you (seats 5, reliable, good gas mileage, built like a tank, looks good, fast, etc.)?

How Well Do You Know Me

Do you keep your car clean or do you allow it to pile up with trash first?

If you and your spouse had two cars, one much nicer than the other, who do you think should drive the newer vehicle? Would it make any difference if only one of you worked?

Do you enjoy going on long road trips as the driver? As the passenger?

Do you find that driving with your partner is pleasant or stressful?

Do you personally wash and wax your car? How often?

If your partner asked you to slow down or to drive more carefully, would you?

Past & Future

Learning more about your partner's past will often give you an understanding on what makes them who they are today. And knowing their visions for the future lets you know where they are heading (those who don't have any goals probably aren't going very far).

What were you teased about when you were younger? How did that make you feel? Did you tease others?

Have you ever performed on stage in a band, a play or other performance? How did it make you feel?

Did you ever hang out with the wrong crowd in school? Did your parents know about it?

Were you a good teenager or did you give your parents a lot of grief?

Were you always getting in trouble for a particular thing when you were a child?

Did you ever run away from home? If so, why?

What school sports and activities did you participate in up through college? What goals do you have for your marriage?

Is there anything you feel you must accomplish before you die? What steps do you need to take to achieve these goals?

What are three goals you have for this year?

How Well Do You Know Me

What are your top ten goals for your lifetime?

In what ways does our relationship help and/or hinder the achievement of your goals?

Love, Romance & Date Nights

Ask 100 people for their definitions of love and romance and you will probably get at least a dozen different answers. It is important that you and your partner are speaking the same language. While love and romance often comes easy early in the relationship, it becomes harder to maintain as years go by. Having regular date nights is an excellent way to keep the love and romance in your marriage.

What crazy thing have you done in the name of "love"?

What things have I done that make you question whether or not I love you?

What rituals could be added to our relationship on a daily, weekly, monthly and yearly basis that would help us to remain close?

Do you think you are a romantic person? Could you convince a jury?

Would you like it if your partner massaged you without expecting any sexual outcome? If you don't give your mate massages, why not?

What sort of physical affection do you think is appropriate in public? Does it matter whether or not the couple is married?

What one thing could we do to improve our dates together?

How do you tend to express love for your sweetheart? (Things you do, Things you say, Gifts you buy, etc.?)

How Well Do You Know Me

Do you think your partner is "romantic"? If not, how could he or she improve? What are some things that your partner has done for you that really made you feel loved?

What's the most romantic thing that's ever been done for you?

What's the most romantic thing you've ever done?

There are many types of love. Can you name some and tell how they are different?

Have you ever written a love letter? Do you save old love letters?

People like to be shown love in different ways. What are some of the ways you like to be shown that someone loves you?

From previous relationships, what was the best date you had? What was the best date we have been on?

In what ways do you like to be romanced?

What is your definition of "romance"?

Is it difficult for you to say "I love you"?

Do you need to hear "I love you" or similar words on a regular basis from your partner?

Friends & Family

Friends and family have the ability to draw the two of you together and they can also pull the two of you apart. When you get married, you create a new family – one that becomes more important than your original family and network of friends. It can be tough when you have known your family and friends for so much longer than your mate.

How do you feel about the way your parents raised you? How did they do a good job and how did they mess up?

What do you think is the common link among all (or at least most) of your friends? (School, Work, Personality, Hobbies, etc.)

Do you have problems letting friendships dissolve when you realize you have little in common? Do you feel obligated to keep close family ties with relatives you would not normally choose to socialize with? Is it ever appropriate to "divorce" yourself from certain family members?

Do you like it when friends feel comfortable enough to drop by unexpectedly?

Who is your least favorite relative? Do you try to avoid him or her?

Do you have a favorite relative? What makes them so special?

Is your family important to you? Why?

Do you think you could live more than six hours away from your parents and/or siblings?

On a typical day/night out with your friends, what do you do?

How Well Do You Know Me

Did you grow up in an ethnic or culturally unique community? What role does it play in your life? Will you want to stay active in that community when you get married?

In what ways do you think your parents could select a better mate for you than you could?

If your family hated the person you were dating and voiced strong opinion against you marrying him or her, would you get married anyway?

How have you changed since high school? What would your high school pals think about you now?

What does my family do that annoys you?

What family traditions did you have growing up? Would you want your children to continue them?

What is the most important thing you learned from your father? What are some other things he taught you?

What makes the difference between a good parent and a great parent?

Do you enjoy hosting out of town guests in your home? If so, how long?

How powerful is peer pressure to you? Do you feel you need to live in a similar fashion as your friends? Did you have problems with peer pressure in your earlier years?

Which family member are you closest to? Has it always been that way?

How Well Do You Know Me

Have you given any thought to how you will take care of your mom and dad when they are older and need assistance?

What is your relationship with your siblings?

What makes the difference between a good husband and a great husband? Good wife and a great wife?

What did you most enjoy doing with your family when you were a kid?

How do you feel about friends, relatives or people in need living in your house for a year?

What's the biggest fight you've had with your family? Has the issue been completely settled?

How often do you see your family? Do you think that's enough or too much?

How have your family been poor role models for relationships?

Did you ever hear or see your parents fighting when you were a child? How did it make you feel?

What is the most important thing you learned from your mother? What are some other things she taught you?

Did one of your parents love you more than the other?

Do you think it is risky or unhealthy for your mate to have a best friend's of the opposite sex?

Do any of your friends have things that make you envious?

How Well Do You Know Me

Which of your friends is most successful? Would you like to have the same level of success?

What positive things have you learned from observing your parents' marriage?

Do you think you are a good influence on your friends or do you think they need you to be a good influence on them? How are they a bad influence?

How long do you think you could stay with my parents before you became unhappy or resentful?

When you are in a serious relationship do you tend to ignore your friends?

Have you ever had friends get married and suddenly lose contact with their single friends? Is that to be expected?

Have you ever had to deal with conflict in you family? How did you do it?

Have your grandparents taught you anything really important or profound?

What is your parents' nationality? Were you raised in that culture or do you know much about it?

Do you like your last name? If you don't like it, would you consider changing it?

If we have children, how often would you like the children to see their grandparents? Do you have any particular concern about the children spending too much time with any of their grandparents or relatives (that are racist, alcoholics, foul-mouthed, ill-tempered, etc.)?

Can you say "no" to your parents when they want you to do something you would prefer not to?

When you get married, do you think there would be any changes in your social circle? Which friendships do you think you would let go and which ones would you add?

If you were married, how would you like to meet new people to socialize with?

Are you currently satisfied with the quality and quantity of friends you have? Why or why not? Early in the dating stage, how strongly do you consider your friends and family's opinion as to whether you should continue seeing someone?

When was the last time you called your Mom, just to tell her you love her? Your Dad?

How often do you call your parents/family members?

Who is your best friend? What about this person makes them so special?

Ideally, what characteristics would your friends have?

What have your friends taught you?

Are you jealous of any of the members of your family? Why?

Conclusion

If you have successfully gone through all the questions in this book with your partner you now know each other better than 99% of the couples on the face of the earth. Either the answers to the questions will have drawn you closer together or they have shown you some areas where your relationship needs some improvement. In many cases, these questions have shown couples that they are not best suited to be life long mates. Indeed that is time and money well spent.

Made in the USA
Monee, IL
14 September 2022